Feb 2017

D1608603

THE LIFE OF
POCAHONTAS

KRISTEN RAJCZAK

PowerKiDS press™

New York

Published in 2017 by The Rosen Publishing Group, Inc.
29 East 21st Street, New York, NY 10010

First Edition

Editor: Sarah Machajewski
Book Design: Katelyn Heinle/Tanya Dellaccio

Photo Credits: Cover (Pocahontas) UniversalImagesGroup/Universal Images Group/Getty Images; cover (background) Anton Foltin/Shutterstock.com; pp. 5, 13 Kean Collection/Getty Images; p. 7 https://en.wikipedia.org/wiki/Powhatan#/media/File:The_Coronation_of_Powhatan_John_Gadsby_Chapman.jpeg; p. 9 Three Lions/Hulton Royals Collection/Getty Images; p. 11 MPI/Archive Photos/Getty Images; p. 15 Archive Photos/Getty Images; p. 17 Print Collector/Hulton Archive/Getty Images; p. 19 https://en.wikipedia.org/wiki/Pocahontas#/media/File:Pocahontas-saves-Smith-NE-Chromo-1870.jpeg; p. 21 https://en.wikipedia.org/wiki/Pocahontas#/media/File:The_Abduction_of_Pocahontas.jpg; p. 23 https://en.wikipedia.org/wiki/Pocahontas#/media/File:Baptism_of_Pocahontas.jpg; p. 25 Universal History Archive/Universal Images Group/Getty Images; p. 27 https://upload.wikimedia.org/wikipedia/commons/9/90/Pocahontas_painting.jpg; p. 29 Jordan McAlister/Moment/Getty Images.

Library of Congress Cataloging-in-Publication Data

Rajczak, Kristen, author.
 The life of Pocahontas / Kristen Rajczak.
    pages cm. — (Native American biographies)
 Includes index.
 ISBN 978-1-5081-4822-7 (pbk.)
 ISBN 978-1-5081-4783-1 (6 pack)
 ISBN 978-1-5081-4818-0 (library binding)
 1. Pocahontas, -1617—Juvenile literature. 2. Powhatan women—Biography—Juvenile literature. 3. Smith, John, 1580-1631—Juvenile literature. I. Title.
 E99.P85R47 2016
 975.501092—dc23
 [B]
                    2015032597

Manufactured in the United States of America

CPSIA Compliance Information: Batch #BS16PK: For Further Information contact Rosen Publishing, New York, New York at 1-800-237-9932

CONTENTS

A STORY OF UNCERTAINTY

The story of Pocahontas's life has been told again and again in books and movies, both fiction and nonfiction. However, although she is one of the best-known Native Americans in American history, the tales of Pocahontas's life are colored by uncertainty. This is partly due to her short life—she was only about 21 years old when she died. It's also because of the conflicting accounts of her life, none of which she had a hand in telling.

For a long time, most knowledge of Pocahontas came from the writings of English captain John Smith. More recently, a book based on the **oral history** of the Mattaponi tribe has provided another look at Pocahontas's life. Together, they paint a picture of a brave woman trying to do the best she could for her people.

The Smith and Mattaponi accounts often tell completely different stories about events in Pocahontas's life. There's no way to know which is more **accurate**.

5

POWHATAN AND HIS PEOPLE

Pocahontas was the daughter of the great Chief Powhatan, or Wahunsenacawh. By the early 1600s, Powhatan joined about 30 groups of Native Americans who lived around Chesapeake Bay and Tidewater Virginia in one powerful **confederacy** with him as their leader. They paid their leader in food and goods that were then shared or traded with the more than 150 towns under his rule.

When the English arrived, Pocahontas's father was an established chief. The English began to call those in his confederacy "Powhatan" after him, even though they belonged to many different groups. Not much is known about Chief Powhatan from before the English arrived. However, he played a big part in the first decade of permanent English settlement in Virginia. Without him, it's unlikely Pocahontas would have been much of a historical figure.

According to many accounts of her life, Pocahontas was Powhatan's favorite daughter.

YOUNG POCAHONTAS

Pocahontas was born around 1596. She was one of many children of Powhatan, who had several wives. Her mother isn't mentioned in historical accounts, and it's thought she may have died in childbirth. Most Powhatan babies lived with their mother's people for childhood, but Pocahontas may not have because of her mother's death.

Even though Pocahontas was the chief's daughter, she would've learned the work of a Powhatan woman. Women took care of homes, children, cooking, and farming. She would've learned how to find **edible** plants and to make baskets and clothing. However, because she was the daughter of the chief, she would've been protected and had a more comfortable lifestyle than other Powhatan women.

Pocahontas would have been considered a woman around age 13 or 14, which meant she was able to marry.

WHAT'S IN A NAME?

WHILE "POCAHONTAS" HAS BECOME A FAMOUS NAME, IT'S NOT THE ONLY ONE SHE WAS KNOWN BY. AT BIRTH, SHE WAS NAMED AMONUTE AND SOMETIMES CALLED MATOAKA. POCAHONTAS WAS A NICKNAME, THAT MEANT "PLAYFUL ONE" OR "**MISCHIEVOUS** ONE." IT MAY HAVE BEEN HER MOTHER'S NAME. AMONUTE FORMALLY CHANGED HER NAME TO POCAHONTAS AT SOME POINT, AND THEN TO REBECCA WHEN SHE LIVED WITH THE ENGLISH.

THE JAMESTOWN SETTLEMENT

Pocahontas was about 10 years old when the first permanent English settlement in North America was established in 1607. Called Jamestown, the colony was founded near where Williamsburg, Virginia, is today. That was right in the middle of Powhatan land.

Not long after the settlers landed, Powhatan warriors attacked them. Had Powhatan wanted to, he likely could have quickly done away with the colonists. Some historians think Powhatan didn't think the English were as big a threat as the other Native American groups in his region who challenged his power. Or, perhaps he thought they would leave soon enough. Whatever the reason Powhatan allowed the English to stay, this first attack may have caused the colonists to be even more wary of the Native Americans.

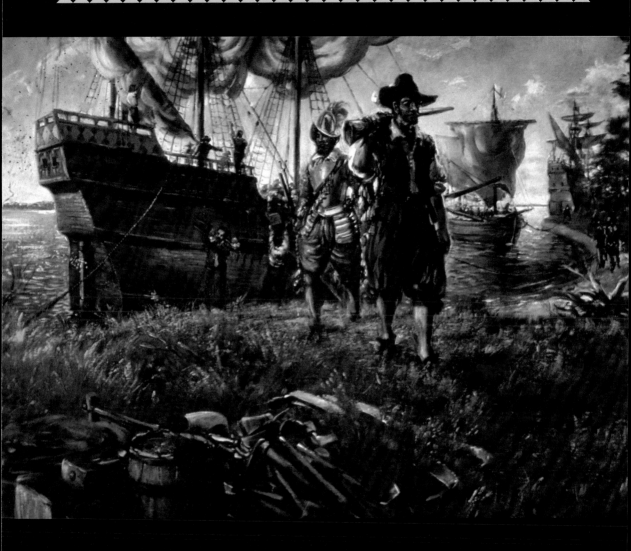

The people of the Powhatan Confederacy and the English had a lot to teach one another, but their encounters weren't always friendly.

POCAHONTAS AND JOHN SMITH

Though Pocahontas was only a child when the Jamestown settlement was founded, there's a famous story about her that's often included in the history of the colony's founding. It comes from the accounts of John Smith, who was a leader at Jamestown.

According to Smith, he was captured by Powhatan's brother, Opechancanough. Smith said he was taken to Powhatan, and his head was pressed against a big stone. Then, a warrior holding a club came toward him. Just before the deathblow, Smith wrote, Pocahontas ran in and saved his life by placing her head over his!

Oddly, the story of Pocahontas saving Smith's life isn't in his journals from the time. It's only included in his later writings about his time in Jamestown. Did this really happen, or did John Smith make it up at a later date? Nobody knows for sure.

Saving John Smith is one of the only specific events of Pocahontas's childhood written about in history books.

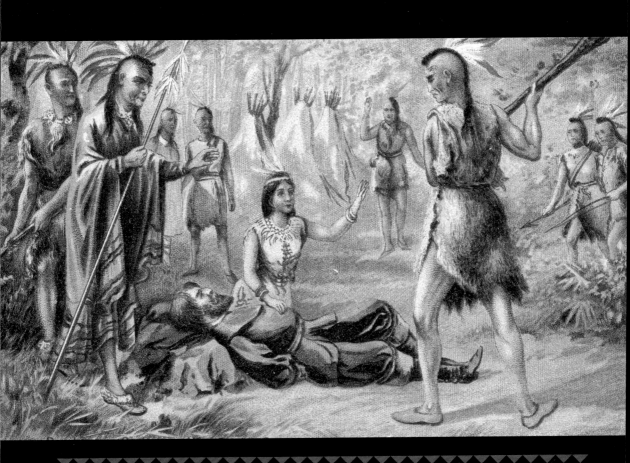

It's possible that Smith made up the story of Pocahontas saving his life. It's also possible that some of it is true, and that he misunderstood what was happening. Smith and Powhatan's meeting could have been a religious ceremony of some kind or a way of accepting Smith into the Powhatans as a leader of the English. Some historians think it's unlikely a child of Pocahontas's age would've attended such an event. Others say her rescue could have been part of the ceremony, and Smith's life was never in danger. He was allowed to leave, unharmed, and go back to Jamestown soon after.

Whatever happened, Pocahontas did meet Smith in the winter of 1607. The two of them were friendly after that.

BELIEVING SMITH

PERHAPS PEOPLE HAVE BELIEVED JOHN SMITH'S **VERSION** OF THE STORY FOR SO LONG BECAUSE THEY FELT HE WAS A TRUSTWORTHY SOURCE. HE ACCURATELY MAPPED MUCH OF THE VIRGINIA COAST AND WROTE A LOT ABOUT THE PEOPLE AND PLACES HE SAW THERE. IN 1608, SMITH BECAME PRESIDENT OF THE JAMESTOWN COLONY AND WORKED TO BUILD UP THE SETTLEMENT. HE WAS A RESPECTED EXPLORER, SO WHY WOULD HE HAVE LIED ABOUT POWHATAN'S DAUGHTER? WE MAY NEVER KNOW.

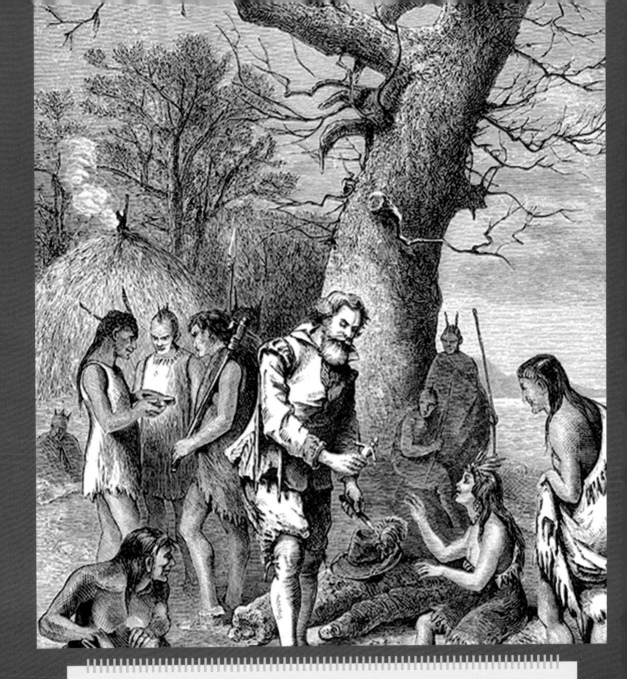

A number of movies have shown Pocahontas and John Smith fall in love. When they met, Smith was almost 28, making him much older than Pocahontas. There was no romantic part to their relationship.

POCAHONTAS AT JAMESTOWN

Pocahontas was an important part of her father's relations with Jamestown. As both a child and the daughter of the chief, Pocahontas's presence was a symbol of peace. She would accompany food and other goods her father gave to the English, who were struggling to survive. Relations between the English and Powhatans were never perfect, even early on, and members of the two groups sometimes took each other prisoner. John Smith wrote that Pocahontas was once in charge of **negotiating** the release of some Powhatan prisoners. Smith said he would only release them to her.

Pocahontas didn't always have such an adult **role** at Jamestown. She played with the young boys who were at the settlement, too, living up to her name by doing cartwheels.

As Powhatan's daughter, Pocahontas would have had warriors with her at Jamestown for protection.

17

By the winter of 1608 and 1609, the dealings between the settlers and the Powhatans had become more and more unfriendly. In addition, a **drought** had greatly reduced the harvest. The Powhatans didn't have as much food to share with the starving English. Soon, Powhatan stopped all gifts and trade with the English.

The settlers continued to ask for food. According to one story, Powhatan sent John Smith a message: If he brought certain English goods, Powhatan would fill Smith's ship with corn. Smith arrived to make the trade, but the talk didn't go well. Powhatan and his family left Smith and the men he brought. Smith wrote that Pocahontas returned at night to warn him that her father was going to kill him.

THE STARVING TIME

THE FOLLOWING WINTER WAS EVEN WORSE FOR THE JAMESTOWN SETTLEMENT. HISTORIANS CALL THE WINTER OF 1609 AND 1610 THE STARVING TIME. ABOUT THREE-QUARTERS OF THE COLONISTS DIDN'T SURVIVE DUE TO LACK OF FOOD OR SICKNESSES CAUSED BY LACK OF FOOD. THE POOR SUPPLIES WERE IN PART DUE TO A POWHATAN **SIEGE** ON THE ENGLISH SETTLEMENT. THE SIEGE LASTED UNTIL MAY 1610, FORCING THE COLONISTS TO EAT SNAKES, CATS, HORSES, AND DOGS. THEY MAY HAVE EVEN EATEN EACH OTHER.

Smith's account also states that Pocahontas saved the life of an English boy living with the Powhatans. This is another of many images of her saving John Smith's life.

KIDNAPPED!

Between 1609 and 1613, Pocahontas didn't visit Jamestown. She married Kocoum, who may have been a lower-ranking warrior commander. Historians guess that Pocahontas married him for love because he wasn't a chief or other high-ranking member of the Powhatan Confederacy. They moved to Kocoum's village, and they may have had a son together.

In 1613, when Pocahontas was 16 or 17, the Powhatans and English were still on bad terms. An Englishman named Sir Samuel Argall thought he might be able to force the Powhatans to work with the English again by kidnapping Pocahontas and holding her until Powhatan returned some English weapons, tools, and prisoners. However, according to some accounts, Powhatan wouldn't turn everything over to Argall. Pocahontas was taken to live in a nearby English settlement called Henrico.

Argall was only able to kidnap Pocahontas with the help of a Patawomeck Indian and his wife. You can see them in the lower left corner of this image of Pocahontas's kidnapping.

WHAT HAPPENED TO KOCOUM?

IN THE POWHATAN **CULTURE**, WOMEN COULD CHOOSE WHOM THEY MARRIED. DIVORCE, OR THE END OF A MARRIAGE, WAS POSSIBLE IF A COUPLE DIDN'T GET ALONG. AFTER POCAHONTAS WAS KIDNAPPED, KOCOUM MAY HAVE CONSIDERED THEIR MARRIAGE OVER BECAUSE IT COULDN'T CONTINUE WITH HER GONE. ACCORDING TO THE MATTAPONI ORAL HISTORY, ARGALL HAD KOCOUM KILLED! IT'S UNCERTAIN WHETHER THIS HAPPENED. BUT, IN POWHATAN CULTURE, DIVORCED PEOPLE WERE EXPECTED TO REMARRY. KOCOUM COULD HAVE SURVIVED AND TAKEN ANOTHER WIFE.

Pocahontas's life changed completely after her kidnapping. She learned English **customs** and to speak their language. Pocahontas also learned about Christianity in order to prepare her for **conversion**.

According to the English account, Pocahontas met John Rolfe during this time. He was a respected colonist who introduced tobacco as a crop in Virginia. The pair fell in love and wanted to get married. The English sent Powhatan a message, and he accepted their union. He sent representatives from their family to attend the wedding.

Following the wedding of John Rolfe and Pocahontas, relations between the Jamestown settlers and Powhatan's people became generally peaceful. They remained so until Powhatan died in April 1618 and for a short time after his death.

THE ORAL HISTORY SAYS...

THE MATTAPONI ORAL HISTORY GIVES A MUCH DIFFERENT PICTURE OF POCAHONTAS'S NEW LIFE WITH THE ENGLISH. FIRST, SHE WAS LED TO BELIEVE HER FATHER WOULDN'T FIGHT FOR HER RELEASE BECAUSE HE NO LONGER LOVED HER. BEING TOLD THIS UPSET POCAHONTAS GREATLY. THE ORAL HISTORY ALSO SAYS POCAHONTAS HAD A HALF-ENGLISH CHILD BEFORE SHE MARRIED JOHN ROLFE AND DIDN'T MARRY HIM OUT OF LOVE, BUT TO BRING PEACE TO HER PEOPLE AND HAVE A FAMILY FOR HER SON.

Pocahontas's conversion to Christianity occurred in 1614. Her Christian name was Rebecca.

TO ENGLAND!

Pocahontas went to England with her husband and baby son, Thomas, in 1616. Other Native Americans joined the Rolfes on the journey, as did Virginia's governor, Thomas Dale. The Virginia Company, the group that gave the money for the founding of Jamestown, paid for the trip. They hoped a visit from a Powhatan "princess" who married an Englishman would make people interested in the colony.

Pocahontas met King James I and Queen Anne. She was also reunited with John Smith, who she had been told was dead. Smith reported that Pocahontas was very emotional about seeing him in England at first. Then, she got angry and told him she was disappointed in how he had treated her father when Powhatan had been so welcoming to Smith.

Pocahontas is presented to
King James I and his court.

After traveling around England for many months, Pocahontas, Rolfe, and their son were planning to go back to Virginia. It was March 1617, and the family had just taken a trip down the Thames River. Pocahontas suddenly became ill and died.

Historians don't agree about how Pocahontas died. She may have had **pneumonia** or another sickness called dysentery, which includes stomach pain and fever. However, the oral history reports that Pocahontas and Rolfe had recently eaten dinner with Sir Argall—and that her death came soon after that. Pocahontas's sister, who was in England with her, told Powhatan she thought Pocahontas had been poisoned! Both stories agree that Pocahontas was buried in a town called Gravesend. Rolfe returned to Virginia and Thomas, who was sickly, stayed in England.

This portrait of Pocahontas was created while she was in England. Her English clothing may have hidden the tattoos Powhatan women often had.

MOVIE CONTROVERSY

IN 1995, DISNEY MADE A CARTOON MOVIE CALLED *POCAHONTAS*. IN IT, A GROWN-UP POCAHONTAS FALLS IN LOVE WITH ENGLISH CAPTAIN JOHN SMITH. SOME NATIVE AMERICAN GROUPS WERE ANGRY THAT THE MOVIE SHOWED A VERY INACCURATE VERSION OF THE STORY. ONE PROBLEM WITH CHANGING THE FACTS OF THE TRUE STORY, SOME SAID, WAS THAT IT SHOWED A MOSTLY HAPPY PICTURE OF EUROPEANS "DISCOVERING" AN UNTOUCHED AMERICAN CONTINENT. IN REALITY, NATIVE AMERICANS HAD LIVED ON THE LAND FOR GENERATIONS AND WERE LATER FORCED OFF IT.

Ætatis suæ 21. Aº. 1616.

A STORY FOR THE AGES

After the deaths of Pocahontas and Powhatan, the strained peace between the Jamestown Colony and the Powhatan Confederacy again crumbled. In 1622, the Powhatans attacked farms around Jamestown, killing more than 300 colonists. The English **retaliated** by poisoning a gift of wine and killed about 200 Native Americans. Violence continued as the colony grew.

Despite these problems, when John Smith wrote about his experiences in Virginia, Powhatan and his daughter were included. In his *Generall Historie of Virginia*, which was published in 1624, Smith tells the story of a young Powhatan girl who saved his life. It was a positive story of the Native Americans living near the new colony. Whether or not it was true, this story has lasted and introduced the mysterious Pocahontas to generations of Americans.

Images of Pocahontas can be found around the country, including this statue in Pocahontas, Iowa.

TIMELINE OF POCAHONTAS AND HER PEOPLE

CA. 1596 The daughter of a Powhatan Chief is [...] originally called Amonute or Matoa[...]

EARLY 1600S Powhatan Confederacy fo[...]

1607 The Jamestown Settlement is founded [...]

1607 Pocahontas meets John Smith. She becom[...] between him, the people of Jamestown, a[...]

1608 John Smith is named president of Jam[...]

1609 Pocahontas warns Smith of a plot to [...]

1609–10 Jamestown colonists experienc[...] worst winters in its history.

ca. 1610 Pocahontas marries Kocou[...] hey may have had [...]

1613 Samuel Argall kidnaps Pocaho[...]

1614 Pocahontas converts to Christianity, changes her name to Rebecca, and marries John Rolfe.

1616 Pocahontas travels to England with Rolfe. She is presented to the king and queen, and spends time traveling around the country.

1617 After a trip on the Thames River, Pocahontas becomes ill and dies.

1618 Powhatan dies.

1622 Violence escalates between Powhatan Confederacy and colonists, straining relations between them.

1624 John Smith publishes his *Generall Historie of Virginia*, which includes his story about Pocahontas.

GLOSSARY

accurate: Free of mistakes.

confederacy: A group of people joined together under one government.

conversion: To change from one set of beliefs to another.

culture: The beliefs and ways of life of a group of people.

custom: A traditional way of doing something.

drought: A long period in which there is little or no rain.

edible: Able to be eaten.

mischievous: Showing a willingness to cause playful trouble.

negotiate: To discuss something in order to make an agreement.

oral history: The past of a group of people passed down by word of mouth.

pneumonia: An illness that affects the lungs.

retaliate: To get back at someone who harmed you.

role: The part someone plays in something.

siege: A time in which warriors or soldiers surround a place in order to take control of it.

version: One form of something.

INDEX

WEBSITES

Due to the changing nature of Internet links, PowerKids Press has developed an online list of websites related to the subject of this book. This site is updated regularly. Please use this link to access the list: www.powerkidslinks.com/natv/poca